For Michael,

with gratitude
for allowing me to
be part of this program,
and thanks for your
friendship.

Ron

5/30/02

/ Raising the Dead \

Raising the Dead

Ron Rash

IRIS PRESS
Oak Ridge, TN
www.irisbooks.com

Cover Photo: Copyright © 2002 by Bill Barley

1st Title Page Photo: Copyright © 1974 by Duke Power

Book Design: Robert B. Cumming, Jr.

/ \

Library of Congress Cataloging-in-Publication Data

Rash, Ron, 1953-
    Raising the dead / Ron Rash.
        p. cm.
    ISBN 0-916078-54-X
1. Appalachian Region, Southern—Poetry. 2. Loss
(Psychology)—Poetry. 3. North Carolina—Poetry. 4. Mountain
life—Poetry. I. Title.
    PS3568.A698 R35 2002
    811'.54—dc21
                            2001006866

ACKNOWLEDGMENTS

Asheville Poetry Review: "Shelton Laurel"

American Literary Review: "Analepsis"

Atlanta Review: "Brightleaf"

Carolina Quarterly: "Under Jocassee," "Beyond"

Chattahoochie Review: "Barn Burning: 1967," "Work, for the Night is Coming," "Burning The Field," "A Homestead on the Horsepasture," "The Dowry"

Cumberland Poetry Review: "Compass Creek"

Greensboro Review: "'Kephart in the Smokies"

Hiram Poetry Review: "Black-eyed Susans"

Mossy Creek Reader: "Deep Water," "In Dismal Gorge"

North Carolina Literary Review: "At Leicester Cemetery"

Oxford American: "The Request"

Passages North: "Fall Creek," "On the Dock," "The Release," "Jocassee, 1916"

Pembroke Magazine: "Spear Point"

Poet Lore: "Taking Down the Lines"

Poetry: "Wolf Laurel"

Quadrant (Australia): "Barbed Wire"

Rattapallax: "The Watch"

Riverrun: "The Search"

Sanctuary: "'Carolina Parakeet"

Sewanee Review: "Calenture," "Death's Harbors," "The Men Who Raised the Dead"

South Carolina Review: "The Vanquished," "Shee-Show," "At Boone Creek Landing," "Tremor," "Bottomland"

Southeast Review: "Watauga County: 1974," "The Debt"

Southern Review: "Whippoorwill," "Madison County: 1934," "The Emerging," "Madison County: June, 1999"

Southwest Review: "Last Service"

Tar River Poetry: "At Reid Hartley's Junkyard"

Virginia Quarterly Review: "Antietam"

Weber Studies: "Speckled Trout"

Yale Review: "In the Barn"

The author wishes to thank family and friends for support while writing these poems. He would also like to thank Tri-County Technical College and Lenior-Rhyne College for providing time to complete this book.

In memory of Jeffrey Charles Critcher

1956-1974

Glendower:
> *I can call spirits from the vasty deep.*

Hotspur:
> *Why, so can I, so can any man.*
> *But will they come when you do call for them?*

— Henry IV, Part One

CONTENTS

I

II

III

I

LAST SERVICE

Though cranes and bulldozers came,
yanked free marble and creek stones
like loose teeth, and then shovels
unearthed coffins and Christ's
stained glass face no longer paned
windows but like the steeple,
piano, bell, and hymnals
followed that rolling graveyard
over the quick-dying streams,
the soon obsolete bridges —
they still congregated there,
wading then crossing in boats
those last Sunday nights, their farms
already lost in the lake,
nothing but that brief island
left of their world as they lit
the church with candles and sang
from memory deep as water
old hymns of resurrection
before leaving that high ground
where the dead had once risen.

UNDER JOCASSEE

One summer morning when
the sky is blue and deep
as the middle of the lake,
rent a boat and shadow
Jocassee's western shoreline
until you reach the cove
that was Horsepasture River.
Now bow your head and soon
you'll see as through a mirror
not a river but a road
flowing underneath you.
Follow that road into
the deeper water where
you'll pass a family graveyard,
then a house and barn.
All that's changed is time,
so cut the motor and drift
back sixty years and remember
a woman who lived in that house,
remember an August morning
as she walks from the barn,
the milking done, a woman
singing only to herself,
no children yet, her husband
distant in the field.
Suddenly she shivers,
something dark has come
over her although
no cloud shades the sun.
She's no longer singing.
She believes someone
has crossed her grave, although
she will go to her grave,
a grave you've just passed over,
wondering why she looked up.

PANTHER TREE

Tracked across Devil's Fork Creek,
treed in a white oak before

men kicked back hounds so wicklight
might be raised first, then rifles

fired to kill the last panther
ever to stalk Jocassee.

Knives then glistened, skinned the cat
that it might banner a barn

stretched out as if still in flight,
while the severed head was placed

between two branches to rise
higher each year no other

panther's cry filled the valley,
the men who killed it coming

each fall when the last leaf fell,
revealed the cat's widening gaze,

what they had once brought to earth
unearthed forever to loom

over their lives like shadow —
shoulders skull-sprung, higher limbs

become sky-raking claws when
wind stirred like fear, like wisdom.

THE VANQUISHED

Even two centuries gone
their absence lingered — black hair
dazzling down a woman's back
like rain, a man's high cheekbones,
a few last names, no field plowed
without bringing to surface
pottery and arrowheads,
bone-shards that spilled across rows
like kindling, a once-presence
keen as the light of dead stars.

THE SEARCH

What hope we had had died by afternoon.
We should have given up, gone home to eat,
left her in the woods. November frost
would keep her well enough till morning came.
The dead have all the time in the world. Besides
she wasn't our kin. She wasn't even white.
Her and her old man had moved up here
twelve years ago. We didn't know from where.
They never told us. They kept to themselves,
farming a hollow far up Painter Creek,
the only colored we had ever known.

Though there'd been times we helped each other out,
racing rain to get hay in a loft,
finding a cow, building a barn or shed,
the things all farmers do to get along.
So he'd come to us when she wandered off
just like she'd done before, except before
he'd always found her, usually at the creek,
or standing in the fields still as a scarecrow.
She'd got so old she was lost inside her mind,
and wasn't going to get home by herself,
so we left our wives, our after-supper fire.

We didn't find her either that first night
our lanterns lighted up the mountainside,
our voices hoarsened — just our voices replied.
At dawn most left, went home to sleep or work.
Four of us decided to stay on.
We took Ezekiel, that was his name,
back to the shack. The women fixed a meal.
He wanted to go but would only slow us down,

so left behind, his face cupped in his hands,
and searched until the sun was just a hint
behind Whiteside Mountain as we climbed
up Wildhog Ridge, the one place left to look,
our heaved-out breaths like smoke in the last light.

We buttoned up our coats and lit the wicks,
swore we'd only search another hour,
swore that several times before we found her,
back against a tree like she'd been waiting.
A harvest moon broke through a patch of clouds.
We raised her in its light and lantern light,
and looked into a face the frost had burned
as white as dogwood blossoms in the spring.
A soft breeze stirred the leaves and then lay down,
the way a weary hound settles to sleep.
It was so quiet. No one seemed to breathe.

Josh Burton held her first, cradled her
against his chest, stumbled down the ridge.
We all took our turn. The women did the rest,
bathed and dressed her, stayed with her till dawn.
We left to get some sleep, not saying much,
thinking of cows to be milked, land to be cleared.

JOCASSEE: 1916

Dam-break, a flood in drought time,
August sun flashing on tin —
a barn roof, all that's above
as two men pass like a cloud
over pasture, boat bow filled
with crowbar and ax, a rope,
for something in that barn lives,
so anchor, hang on the roof,
peel back tin slats, break through beams
before it comes, a stallion
shedding tin's dazzle like scales
as it rises through the roof
like an image opening
inside the mind, born of fire
and waterborne, alive.

FALL CREEK

As though shedding an old skin,
Fall Creek slips free from fall's weight,
clots of leaves blackening snags,
back of pool where years ago
local lore claims clothes were shed
by a man and woman wed
less than a month, who let hoe
and plow handle slip from hands,
left rows half done, crossed dark waves
of bottomland to lie on
a bed of ferns, make a child,
and all the while the woman
stretching both arms behind her
over the bank, hands swaying
wrist-deep in current — perhaps
some old wives' tale, water's pulse
pulsing what seed might be sown,
or just her need to let go
the world awhile, let the creek
wash away every burden
her life had carried so far,
open a room for this new
becoming as her body
flowed around her man like water.

SHEE-SHOW

Shortia galacifolia, commonly known as Oconee Bells.

Michaux called it Shortia
for a London friend, a word
read more than spoken because
white settlers let place and shape
inspire a prettier name,
a rich feel of syllables
rung off the tongue, merging two
cultures for once without blood,
though now so long after those
namegivers have vanished like
what was here, I remember
the Cherokee word, the smooth
surface of its cadence, how
it promised coming water.

ON THE KEOWEE

Three days searchers worked below
rock-leaps her feet had not bridged,
men trolling grabbling hooks through
suck hole and blue hole, bamboo
poles jabbing the backs of falls
before the high sheriff told
her folks there was but one way,
so Jake Poston came, his poke
bulging with a snapper's weight,
its head a jawed fist, mossed shell
big as a washpan, fishhook
deep-barbed in the webbed back foot,
the shank's eye knotted with line
thick as guitar string. He kicked
it off the bank, let out line
like a leash as the snapper
wandered river floor, then stopped,
and Jake just nodded, the men
wading on in. No one spoke
of the gashes in her throat,
or of why he hadn't cut
that line afterward, had slung
thirty pounds of turtle on
his back, headed downriver
to the cabin where no wife
set his table, where no meat
yet simmered in the kettle.

At Boone Creek Landing

Forty yards out, my friend says,
right hand raised as if to lift
Fort Prince George off the lake floor,
reveal a valley, the creek
old topo maps show once ran
outside its walls. Inside me
streams blood merging here the night
a captain named Candler wed
Mary Boone. Soon they left for
North Carolina where they lie
among others who passed on
part of themselves that I might
arrive like a long-delayed
wedding guest to this shore,
their currents of blood carried
above what water buried.

Deep Water

The night smoothes out its black tarp,
tacks it to the sky with stars.
Lake waves slap the bank, define
a shoreline as one man casts
his seine into the unseen,
lifts the net's pale bloom, lets spill
of threadfin fill the live well.
Soon that squared pool of water
flickers as if a mirror,
surfaces memory of when
this deep water was a sky.

II

COMPASS CREEK

Wading across he had lost
his handful of direction,
no choice but follow the creek's
slide and leap downstream and then

a stream of cabin smoke where
the creek slowed, veined a river,
at the door as if waiting
a daughter and her mother.

Three winters away from Wales,
here was what he had searched for:
bottomland, water, a wife.
He traded sweat for supper.

He called his son Aneirin,
renamed the French Broad the Wye.
Soon his son went by Andy.
Only his creek name survived,

named that first evening he held
the daughter's hand as they climbed
slick rocks to where he had lost
what neither wanted to find.

WATAUGA COUNTY: 1803

Night falling, river rising
into the cabin, a hound
howling on the porch, and then
an unbuckling from bank roots,
no time to lantern children
up to loft or higher ground
as the cabin, current-caught,
filled like a trough before lodged
on a rock, and when dawn brought
neighbors and kinfolk the hound
still howled on the porch, allowed
no one to enter until
shot dead by a flintlock pressed
against its head so men might
drag out those drowned in the harsh
covenant of that failed ark.

In Dismal Gorge

The lost can stay lost down here,
in laurel slicks, false-pathed caves.
Too much too soon disappears.

On creek banks clearings appear,
once homesteads. Nothing remains.
The lost can stay lost down here,

like Tom Clark's child, our worst fears
confirmed as we searched in vain.
Too much too soon disappears.

How often this is made clear
where cliff-shadows pall our days.
The lost can stay lost down here,

stones scattered like a river
in drought, now twice-buried graves.
Too much too soon disappears,

lives slip away like water.
We fill our Bibles with names.
The lost can stay lost down here.
Too much too soon disappears.

THE RELEASE

In those last moments before
the platter of salt and dirt
lay on his stomach, wax-light
had waved across a mute heart,
his son waited by the bed.
Raised to believe the soul left
the body with its last breath,
he listened for death's rattle,
then pressed his lips like a kiss
to his father's lips, and took
into his mouth the breath that
had given him breath, a life
distilled to one stir of air
soft as moth wings against palms,
held a moment, then let go.

WHIPPOORWILL

The night Silas Broughton died
neighbors at his bedside heard
a dirge rising from high limbs
in the nearby woods, and thought
come dawn the whippoorwill's song
would end, one life given wing
requiem enough — were wrong,
for still it called as dusk filled
Lost Cove again and Bill Cole
answered, caught in his field, mouth
open as though to reply,
so men gathered, brought with them
flintlocks and lanterns, then walked
into those woods, searching for
death's composer, and returned
at first light, their faces lined
with sudden furrows as though
ten years had drained from their lives
in a mere night, and not one
would say what was seen or heard,
or why each wore a feather
pressed to the pulse of his wrist.

ANTIETAM

The feast huddle explodes when I approach.
A gray fox remains, whitening to bone.
The risen wait in the limbs above
for me to glance the marker, pass on.
And I imagine their ancestors
descending the day after battle,
settling as soft and easy as ashes,
a shuddering quilt of feather and talon.

Locals swore each anniversary
those death-embracers found the way back,
gathered by some avian memory
to turn September branches black
as they hunched in rows like a regiment —
clear-eyed, voiceless, and vigilant.

SHELTON LAUREL

Sister, I have come to understand
the world will have its way with us despite
what we might wish, or once believed. Last week
I watched our neighbors die like snakes. Gut-shot,
then hacked with hoes until their moaning ceased.
Shelton's youngest son was one of them,
just thirteen years old. His eyes met mine,
but like his father and brothers didn't speak.
It was past words by then but still I thought
of all the times the five of us had shared
a hunting camp, spun lies at Allen's Store,
better times before we let this war
settle like a vulture in these hills,
a vulture never sated. Though I aimed
my rifle to the right it didn't matter,
others found the mark with lead or hoe.
And when it ended the sun burned in the sky
like any other day. The French Broad still
flowed southward down to Asheville. In the trees
fox squirrels chattered, wrens still sang their song.
By noon the snow had turned from white to red.
Our sergeant danced like a dervish on the grave,
vowed he'd push them deeper into hell.
And I was there, dear sister, I was there,
and still feel I am there although I hide
miles away, deep inside this cavern
and write this letter with what light is left
in one last stub of candle, light enough
to get this letter written, bring to you,
leave it by your pillow while you sleep,
then make my way back here where I will stay.
A branch runs through this cavern, in it trout

whose eyes are blind from years of too much dark.
I envy them for all they haven't seen,
and maybe with enough time I might too
cease to see these things I tell you of,
that drape upon my soul like heavy shackles,
and then return to you, resume a life
stilled like the hands of a broken pocket watch
beside a stream bank deep in Shelton Laurel.

The Dowry

No Virginia truce could end
what had spread like crown fire to
the farthest shut-in, back cove
of Madison County, war
made tribal as cliff-dwellers
fought valley neighbors. Blood spilled
but enough bad blood remained
to fill hearts for years, and when
Jake Shelton came to the door
of Colonel Candler's study,
asked for the hand of Jenny,
the Colonel raised an empty
gray sleeve in answer, vowed no
homemade yankee would ever
win his daughter's hand until
what he'd lost to a sniper
filled that sleeve again, for months
that missing limb his reply
to pleas of wife and daughter,
kinsman and preacher who spoke
in vain of time's healing balm,
until one April evening
Jake Shelton brought the Colonel
an offering — gauze-wrapped, balanced
on his left palm as though on
a pair of scales, the right wrist
blood-staunched by a lover's knot.

BLACK-EYED SUSANS

The hay was belt-buckle high
when rain let up, three days' sun
baked stalks dry, and by midday
all but the far pasture mowed,
raked into windrows, above
June sky still blue as I drove
my tractor up on the ridge
to the far pasture where strands
of sagging barbed wire marked where
my land stopped, church land began,
knowing I'd find some grave-gift,
flowers, flag, styrofoam cross
blown on my land, and so first
walked the boundary, made sure what
belonged on the other side
got returned, soon enough saw
black-eyed susans, the same kind
growing in my yard, a note
tight-folded tied to a bow.
Always was all that it said,
which said enough for I knew
what grave that note belonged to.
I knew as well who wrote it,
she and him married three months
when he died, now always young,
always their love in first bloom,
too new to life to know life
was no honeymoon. Instead,
she learned that lesson with me
over three decades, what fires
our flesh set early on cooled
by time and just surviving,
and learned why old folks called it

getting hitched, because like mules
so much of life was one long row
you never saw the end of,
and always he was close by,
under a stone you could see
from the porch, wedding picture
she kept hid in her drawer,
his black-and-white flashbulb grin
grinning at me like he knew
he'd made me more of a ghost
to her than he'd ever be.
There at that moment — that word
in my hand, his grave so close,
if I'd had a shovel near
I'd have dug him up right then,
hung his bones up on the fence
like a varmint, made her see
what the real was, for memory
is always the easiest
thing to love, to keep alive
in the heart. After a while
I laid the note and bouquet
where they belonged, never spoke
a word about it to her
then or ever, even when
she was dying, calling his
name with her last words. Sometimes
on a Sunday afternoon
I'll cross the pasture, make sure
her stone's not starting to lean,
if it's early summer bring
black-eyed susans for her grave,
leave a few on his as well,
for soon enough we'll all be
sleeping together, beyond
all things that ever mattered.

CALENTURE

Delirious sailors thought
the sea a green field and walked
into water, so amazed
when what had seemed firm gave way —
a tropical ailment, one
my uncle suffered, not on
ocean but island, far from
all he had known, strange flora,
air thick as oil, give of white
sand with each step he knew might
be his last, and trained his eyes
to sea during day's last light
that he might be deceived and
find green fields, Appalachian
hills unfolding in waves so
he could believe himself home,
the war a dream, and only
then would he drift toward sleep.

Wolf Laurel

Tree branches ice-shackled, ground
hard as an anvil, three sons
and a father leave the blaze
huddled around all morning,
wade snow two miles where they cross
Wolf Laurel Creek, poke rifles
in rock holes, cliff leans hoping
to quarry what's killed five sheep,
but no den found as the ridge
sips away the gray last light
of winter solstice, and they
head back toward home, the trail
falling in blur-dark; and then
the father falls too, eyes locked,
wrist unpulsed, the sons without
lantern, enough lingering light,
know they must leave him or risk
all of them lost, know what waits
for death in that place, so break
a hole in Wolf Laurel's ice,
come back at first light to find
the creek's scab of cold covered
with snow-drift, circling paw prints
brushed away that sons might see
a father's face staring through
the ice as through a mirror.

III

SPECKLED TROUT

Water-flesh gleamed like mica:
orange fins, red flankspots, a char
shy as ginseng, found only
in spring-flow gaps, the thin clear
of faraway creeks no map
could name. My cousin showed me
those hidden places. I loved
how we found them, the way we
followed no trail, just stream-sound
tangled in rhododendron,
to where slow water opened
a hole to slip a line in,
and lift as from a well bright
shadows of another world,
held in my hand, their color
already starting to fade.

In the Barn

The tin roof folded its wings
above my cousin and me
that day the barn mouth darkened,
swallowed its green tongue before
we filled the last stall with straw.
Thunder lumbered up the gorge,
then a sound like berries dropped
in a pail as tin and wood
creaked and wept, afternoon fell
toward an early night, the last
swallow settled in its nest.
We settled as well, let straw
pillow our heads as rain tucked
its loud hush tighter around us.
My cousin lay on his back,
eyes closed, hands on chest as though
already getting ready
for a wake eight years away.

ABOVE GOSHEN CREEK

Rain hard as a waterfall
all morning, by afternoon
Goshen Creek overbanking,
river deep where we dangle
just above, trusting nails
our grandfather drove before
we were born as water slaps
planks a little more loose, sucks
beams under another inch,
and although he is the one
who can't swim I lose our dare,
watch from solid ground as he
stands there between earth and sky
when water crests, oak slats slip
and shudder beneath his feet.

BARN BURNING: 1967

What was left cast no shadow
but was shadow: a black square
of absence laid like a quilt
on the pasture, not even
smoke left by first light, although
still lingering in the air
like a bitter aftertaste,
tobacco burned too early.
A photograph snapped that day
soon became a talisman,
as if the camera captured
flame forever on that farm,
and when they'd weathered that hard
mountain winter something more —
proof that disaster might be
framed by time to fit inside
rows of happier events
whenever the Bible-thick
album sprawled its black and white
backward-turning calendar
across the kitchen table,
and my uncle saw himself
standing alone in the past,
shoulders hunched, eyes dark and cold
as the ashes at his feet.
A man who gets through a time
mean as that need not have fears
of something worse, he would say.
He said that for seven years.

Work, For the Night Is Coming

The tobacco leaves blacken,
root deeper in dark but he
will not follow his father
from the field, not until this
end row is finished with what
light windows from the farmhouse,
where supper cools on the stove,
death-clothes scarecrow a bedpost
as the clock hands spread like wings,
widen this moment he tops
his last plant, becomes a part
of the night before he folds
his barlow knife and walks back
up the row, fingers brushing
the future's gold-ripening —
curing tongues of burley hung
from barn rafters, the harvest
his father will reap alone.

The Debt

We want him to have the best,
they told Barney Hampton as
he led them to a room where
coffins lay open on shelves
like traps waiting to be sprung,
but because he'd always been
an honest man, and because
he knew how little cabbage
and tobacco brought even
in good years, Barney Hampton
passed copper, stainless steel, stopped
where he could make his pitch for
wood's varnished solidity,
but my uncle and aunt said
what they'd said before, then spent
half a decade stooped in fields
so each fall one more ticket
in the coupon book might be
torn out to pay for what they'd
sown deeper than any seed.

WATAUGA COUNTY: 1974

Cold rain, fog thick as gravestone,
six outstretched hands, one hand mine
as I stand with older kin,
await the undertaker's
tight-lipped nod before I lift
what is left, a body more
light than I had imagined,
so light the casket glides like
a boat on currents of white,
as though what is held holds me
above the earth-door he must
enter alone, the right hand
I feared might not raise him now
not wanting to let him down.

BEYOND

This fall night my uncle leaves
bed's warmth for a harvest moon's
thin blanket of light, a hearth
stoked with dry creekdrift. Below
his prize black and tan's stark cry
echoes far down in Dismal's
laurel hells, working its way
back across White Rock Ridge, past
Carl Triplett's corn field, then west
toward church-shadowed stones, one grave
whose dirt has yet to settle.
Dawn-ash and frost coat the ground,
the gorge surfaces before
my uncle leans on a swell
of oak leaf, lets his eyes close
as the hound crosses Goshen,
strikes a fresh trail.

BURNING THE FIELD

My uncle lights the rag fuse
doused with diesel fuel and heaves,
bottle arcing like a flare
before it shatters on ground
between us, flame-spill spreading
like bright roots from middlefield
to the firebreak banks harrowed
that dawn, the banks we vigil
that no spark leap that orange weave
and waver squared in five acres
like a live quilt dying quick
as flame withers; then a gray
smolder like fog rising off
a river, what I walk through
to join my uncle, and now
three decades later wonder
what he saw that afternoon
coming from the other side,
smoke-wreathed, wearing a jacket
passed on, familiar.

AT REID HARTLEY'S JUNKYARD

To enter we find the gap
between barbed wire and briars,
pass the German Shepherd chained
to an axle, cross the ditch
of oil black as a tar pit,
my aunt compelled to come here
on a Sunday after church,
asking me when her husband
refused to search this island
reefed with past catastrophes.
We make our way to the heart
of the junkyard, cling of rust
and beggarlice on our clothes,
bumpers hot as a skillet
as we squeeze between car husks
to find in this forever
stilled traffic one Ford pickup,
tires stripped, radio yanked out,
driver's door open. My aunt
gets in, stares through glass her son
looked through the last time he knew
the world, as though believing
like others who come here she
might see something to carry
from this wreckage, as I will
when I look past my aunt's ruined
Sunday dress, torn stockings, find
her right foot pressed to the brake.

Spear Point

No time to exchange one set
of grave clothes for another,
so my kinsman rests his back
on the back steps, shovel laid
across lap like a rifle,
as though to guard the hole he,
three other men have opened,
waits there while we fill pews,
sing and pray inside, and still
on those steps as pall bearers
bring from the church what brings us
through this gate where lambs pasture
under the gaze of angels.
My kinsman does not join
our huddle across the rows
where we soil our hands, begin
what he will finish. Only
when the preacher says amen
does he let go the shovel,
make his way through that acre
of granite stubbed like clearcut,
offer me words, then what weights
his blistered palm — a spear point
lifted from my father's grave.

IV

THE EMERGING

Cabbage heads piled like slaughter
in the truck bed as he bumps
and jolts out of the field, stops
at the farmhouse to pick up
his wife and daughter, the boy
left behind to worm burley,
the truck halfway to Hickory
when the radio warns what
is coming, may already
have come, and back in the field
what is heard first is silence:
bullfrogs in pond reeds pausing,
crows voiceless as they lift for
deepest woods, and the boy's eyes
lift up as well, and he sees
a half-drawn curtain of dark
lowering the sky until
earth and sky swirl into one
black funnel leaping Ben Greene's
cow pasture, Laurel Fork Creek,
before swerving east, the field where
the boy runs for a shelter
of water, not wood, takes one
last gasp in the shallows, then
disappears, and when sister
and parents arrive they find
no farmhouse, just six stone steps
leading to a vanished door.
Arising out of the pond
a thing like some primal dream
of what we once were — mud-fleshed,
moving on four limbs, then two,
slowly becoming human.

KEPHART IN THE SMOKIES

The morning woods smolder with fog,
the damp, black leaves slick underfoot.
Horace Kephart follows the prong
that pools and falls in Clingman's shadow,

merges soon with Hazel Creek,
loses altitude and then
becomes the Little Tennessee
to flow against the continent,

toward the nation's center where
he's left six children and a wife,
mapped and compassed a way to here,
found this place to lose himself.

Hungover, cotton-mouthed, he pauses,
his hands like prayer to hold the water.
Trembling its cold against his teeth,
he wishes it were something stronger.

BARBED WIRE

New strung, it sparks a live wire
when sun hits right, and can be
thumbed like guitar string, its tune
pure country twang, but given
enough time rain rusts metal,
fence posts wobble like loose teeth,
barbed wire burrows in laurel
and goldenrod before found
by fisherman or hunter.
As I found it once, deep in
the Smokies when something latched
to my calf — coil of old strands
not quite elemented back
into ground ore, and though I searched
no chimney-spill or hearthstone,
no sign but rusty fence-thorns
of one whose hammer tapped out
a claim on this land traveling
through bright lines from post to post,
traveling time to a moment
one man's tenuous hold on
the earth snagged like a memory
surfaced long after, time-dulled,
still able to draw blood.

THE REQUEST

Because her sons gave their word
to honor her dying words —
that she rest among kinfolk
before night fell — they hurried
a coffin out of barn slats,
a scavenge of nails while snow
silenced the hollow, knee-deep
by noon when the last nail nailed
closed the lid and she burdened
two sons' shoulders, another
dragging shovel and mattock
as they crossed Laurel Fork Creek,
over Crow Ridge onto land
owned by a cousin who rode
horseback to fetch a preacher
while they staggered on through snow,
another field, and appeared
from a distance as if men
hanging to a capsized boat,
as they printed one more ridge,
then through the iron gate where
they laid her grave-house among
the blind stones as the preacher
read quick with what light still sparsed
that gray landscape and sons pressed
hats to hearts like poultices,
stamped feet against frozen ground
they would enter before her —
the hard work yet to be done.

Madison County: 1934

He knew what it could not be:
stray dog or fox — on the straw
no spray of blood and feather,
no yellow slobber of yolk.
Small loss, the few eggs taken,
but loss enough in hard times
when springhouse shelves too often
emptied before spring, so he
knotted fish line to a stob,
jabbed hook in an egg to catch
the chicken snake he believed
the thief, and when dawn came found
no snake but a neighbor's child
hunched in a corner, her cheek
opened like a mouth, the barb
unrelenting as hunger.

BRIGHTLEAF

A path once smoothed this creek edge —
limb cuts, uproot, laurel slash,
passage enough to get corn,
tobacco to Boone, though now
the way is blazed by water
I have rockstepped and waded
into a gorge that narrows
like a book slowly closing,
what sunfall cliff-snagged, leaf-seined,
a place named for what it was:
Dismal, Shut In, where I find
family lore confirmed, a squared
plot of slant land, full acre
of white petals surrounding
chimney stub once homestead. Here
a new bride planted hundreds
of dogwoods, so coming springs
branches flared with white blossoms,
waking an orchard of light
against that bleak narrative
of place name, a life scratched out
on ground as much rock as dirt.
Decades passed as she raised what
might look from distant summit
like a white flag unfurled, though
anything but surrender.

At Leicester Cemetery

Six feet below our feet the dead
will not argue or confirm
this ancestral gossip.
Pure Cherokee, my cousin says,
but Baptist so no one cared.
And what of this one? I ask,
pointing to his closest kin.
He killed a man, then schemed
to marry the dead man's widow.
Scandal has weathered to dust
as we acknowledge his rashness
with a smile, move to another plot,
just a first name, the rest
time-swept from the creek rock.
Lost, my cousin says. *I can't*
find her in county records
or family Bibles. It's like
she never lived. We walk back,
pass again men with shovels
who finish what has brought
us back to this high country.
You can see forever from here,
my cousin says. We look west,
eyes bridging French Broad River,
the mountains leveling out
becoming east Tennessee
before they rise again, distant
against an even more distant sky.

COKE BOX

To get there, follow a road
rarely traveled anymore,
the blacktop pocked with pot holes,
scrub oak gnawing the shoulders,
left like a dry riverbed
after the four-lane was built.
Pull over where gas pumps stand
like old diving gear, globe-faced,
barnacled with rust. Barngray
arthritic planks raise a room
thick-shadowed, felt before seen:
floorboards slick with linseed oil,
breeze of ceiling fan, the store's
slow emergence like something
brought up from deep water,
and when all's surfaced it's there,
the lidded long metal trough
you open like a coffin
before plunging half an arm
in ice shards thick as gravel,
grabbling for glass, the dark
sugared water you will raise
to lips, swallow, that you might
imagine forty years back,
a man cancer-caught, AWOL
from his death bed, from women
who thought they'd hidden the truck
keys well enough. Close your eyes,
taste what he tasted, a cold
sweet longing slaked, imagine
his hand closing the coke box,
and know this is why you've come.

Madison County: June, 1999

Where North Carolina locks
like a final puzzle piece
into eastern Tennessee,
old songs of salvation rise
through static on Sunday night
in this mountain county where
my name echoes on gravestones
dimmed by time like the evening
a kinsman held fire, let it lick
his palm like a pet before
he raised that hand so we might
see providence as his tongue
forged a new language bellowed
in a pentecostal blaze.
That is all I remember:
an unburned hand, those strange words,
what came before or after
on that long ago Sunday
dark as beyond the headlights
as I practice smaller acts
of faith on hill crests, blind curves,
and though my life lies elsewhere
some whisper inside urges
another destination,
as if that unburned hand were
raised in welcome, still might lead
me to another state marked
by no human boundary,
where my inarticulate
heart might finally find voice
in words cured by fire, water.

The Wolves in the Asheville Zoo

Fog grazing among the trees,
and they herd with it, become
whispers of movement until
one bares its throat, then silence
as though pausing for answer
from cliff cave or laurel den
vacant twelve decades — and I
pause too, imagine the first
of my name in this county,
rock and wood raised on a ridge,
wind swaying the boards like waves
as if still inside the ship
sailing from land where wolfpacks
vanished far back as fire-drakes,
denned in blood-memory until
given voice one mountain night
as oak slats rattle like bones,
the hearth's last log cools to ash
gray as his eyes as he pokes
charwood for some nub of light.

The Watch

Almost like a scythe, the sweep
of mesh through creek-pool, that slow
harvest of dace and crayfish,
the homemade seine held between
my brother and me, worked deep
in each undercut, sinkers
scraping white sand like a rake,
and this morning a sudden
bowing, then give, bringing up
a gold watch three decades dropped
from our grandfather's pocket,
lost in his field, freshet-swept
to this pool some longback spring.
My knife blade pries open time
like a clam, water spilling
out lost hours, and though I try
with shake and stem wind to rouse,
hands do not move, remain still
at six-thirty, one placed on
the other like dead man's hands.

V

BARTRAM LEAVES JOCASSEE

So easy to believe he
sensed the lake's coming that day
he climbed Oconee Mountain,
cast a last look back before
descending into Georgia:
The mountainous wilderness
appearing regularly,
undulating as the great
ocean after a tempest.

It's called Station Mountain now,
the place he stood, where I stand,
look back as well, and because
history is sometimes more
than irony, imagine
this restless Quaker followed
the land's slow falling away
until distance disappeared,
and he glimpsed something beyond
what even time could fathom.

CAROLINA PARAKEET

Though once plentiful enough
to pulse an acre field, green
a blue sky, they were soon gone,
whole flocks slaughtered in a day,
though before forever lost
found last here, in these mountains
so sparsely settled a man
late as 1860 might
look up from new-broken land
and glimpse that bright vanishing.

Taking Down the Lines

They tore the telephone lines
out of the earth like unhealed
stitches, poles and wires hauled off
through which voices had once flowed
across Jocassee like freshets
crisscrossing, running backward
into far coves where one phone
might be shared by five families.
In those lines was sediment
of births and sicknesses, deaths,
love vows and threats, all passed on
mouth to mouth, vital as breath
before silenced in lake-dim
currents of lost connections.

A Homestead on the Horsepasture

Those last days he stayed to watch
water tug his farm under
one row at a time, so slow
his eyes snagged no memory
of what was lost, no moment
he could say *I saw it end.*
When little else showed but what
his own hands had raised he soaked
house and barn with kerosene,
shattered a lantern, and as
it burned the taste of ashes
filled his mouth until nothing
remained but what he'd corbeled
out of creek stone he would leave
for the water to reclaim.

BOTTOMLAND

No corn summered green and tall
across Cane Creek's bottomland
that last August. What rose there
was the lake's slow becoming,
though scarecrows stayed like totems
giving loss human measure
each day their stakes sank deeper
like faultless divining rods,
and when October's orange
harvest moon blossomed they stalked
those vanished fields, raised arms spread
like arms of the forsaken.

TREMOR

Weight of water was what caused
cups to shiver in cupboards,
cows to pause, Duke Power claimed,
but those who once lived there
thought otherwise, spoke of lives
so rooted in the valley
some part of their lives lingered:
breeze of sickle combing wheat,
stir of hearth-kettle, the tread
of mule across broken ground,
long ago movements breaking
across time like a fault line.

ANALEPSIS

Fishermen have heard it years,
a wailing from deep water
nights the wind settles, the moon
trembles on the lake as if
light not falling but rising,
as if some things cannot be
forever hidden but must
surface — as believers claim
who remember two creek stones
that marked a life's shallow length,
name and date weathered away,
no other graves, as if that
one grief was enough to fill
a whole meadow, forgotten
those days the other dead rose
cradled in live arms before
returned to earth. So on nights
a wet moon rises it wakes
this child who cries to be held,
gives voice to the underneath
of water, the lost unnamed
dawn-calmed by the dam's pale hand.

DEATH'S HARBORS

Where the power company
evicted the quick, the dead,
dive with paned eyes so you may
have a believer's vision —
the long-anticipated
airlift of souls, that rising
like the breath bubbles rising
from your mouthpiece as you fall
like a man parachuting
into a dream, and you wake
where gravestones fin the lake floor,
where dead rested before raised
three decades ago. The holes
their bodies filled have not filled,
death's harbors still vacant. When
you ascend through swirls of shad,
each silver crown breaks apart
around your brow like star-fall.

THE DAY THE GATES CLOSED

We lose so much in this life.
Shouldn't some things stay, she said,
but it was already gone,
no human sound, the poplars
and oaks cut down so even
the wind had nothing to rub
a whisper from, just silence
rising over the valley
deep and wide as a glacier.

BEYOND THE DOCK

Some stars, quarter slice of moon,
but mainly dark, as the dock
creaks and sways like a cradle.
I lie down, shoulder to wood,
cheek on my arm, my ear close
to the rough boards and I hear
lake waves slosh against clay banks,
low whisper of willow oak.
Soon something else, boat motor
purling closer, then shut off,
drifting the deeper water
somewhere out beyond this dock
where my ear leans to the wood
as to a door while a man
and woman convey no words,
only a tone — urgency,
then an image when match-flare
sparks a lantern, making more
dark than all else a female
silhouette, the outstretched palm
letting something slip free, then
the hand spread to the lantern
like a magician proving
the coin is gone before
flame sifts from globe-glass like sand,
expires as the motor coughs,
and they leave, leaving some small
piece of two lives that needed
to fall forever away
in a reservoir so vast
it could bury a valley.

The Men Who Raised the Dead

If they had hair it was gray,
the backs of their hands wormy
currents of blue veins, old men
the undertaker believed
had already lost too much
to the earth to be bothered
by what they found, didn't find,
brought there that May afternoon
dogwood trees bloomed like white wreaths
across Jocassee's valley.

They took their time, sought the shade
when they tired, let cigarettes
and silence fill the minutes
until the undertaker
nodded at his watch, and they
worked again, the only sound
the rasp and suck of shovels
as they settled deeper in graves
twice-dug, sounding for the thud
of struck wood not always found —
sometimes something other, silk
scarf or tie, buckle, button
nestled in some darker earth,
enough to give a name to.

One quit before they were done,
lay down as if death were now
too close to resist, and so
another stepped in his grave,
finished up, but not before
they shut his eyes, laid him with
all the others to be saved
if not from death, from water.

NOTES

Jocassee is the Cherokee word for a valley in the South Carolina mountains. In the early 1970s, despite fervent opposition by the valley's inhabitants, Duke Power Company built a dam to create Jocassee Reservoir. Both the living and the dead were evicted, for hundreds of graves were dug up and their contents reburied in cemeteries outside the valley. The reservoir reached full water capacity in 1974. In Cherokee *Jocassee* means "place of the lost."

Shee-Show: The Cherokee believed the flower's bloom a sign drought was about to end. The French botanist André Michaux traveled through Jocassee Valley in 1788.

The Release: *North Carolina Folklore,* Volume I, Frank C. Brown. "The corpse is stretched on a board. On it is placed a platter of salt and earth. The salt is an emblem of the immortal spirit, the earth of the flesh."

Kephart in the Smokies: Horace Kephart left his wife and children to live alone in the North Carolina mountains. He played a major role in the creation of the Smoky Mountains National Park.

Bartram Leaves Jocassee: The quote is from William Bartram's *Travels*. Bartram traveled through Jocassee Valley in 1775

—Photo by Jeff Daniel Marion

ABOUT THE AUTHOR

Ron Rash grew up in Boiling Springs, North Carolina. He graduated from Gardner-Webb College and Clemson University. He now lives in Clemson, South Carolina, with his wife and two children. He teaches English at Tri-County Technical College, and he teaches poetry in the M.F.A. program at Queens College in Charlotte, North Carolina.

In 1987 his fiction won a General Electric Younger Writers Award, and in 1994 he was awarded an NEA Poetry Fellowship. He was awarded the Sherwood Anderson Prize in 1996. His poetry and fiction have appeared in a number of journals, including *Poetry, Yale Review, Oxford American, New England Review, Southern Review, Shenandoah* and *Sewanee Review*. He is the author of four previous books: *The Night the New Jesus Fell to Earth* and *Casualties*, both collections of stories, and *Eureka Mill* and *Among the Believers*, both collections of poetry.

Þ

This book was typeset in Sabon. A descendant of the types of Claude Garamond, Sabon was designed by Jan Tschicold in 1964 and jointly released by Stempel, Linotype, and Monotype foundries. The roman design is based on a Garamond specimen printed by Konrad F. Berner, who was married to the widow of another printer, Jacques Sabon. The italic design is based on types by Robert Granjon, a contemporary of Garamond's.

The cover photograph of sunset over the Jocassee Reservoir was taken by South Carolina photographer, Bill Barley, around 1984. The photograph of the Jocassee Dam on the 1st title page is derived from a color aerial photograph taken shortly after the reservoir reach full level in 1974. It was generously provided by the photo archive of Duke Power.

♾ The paper in this book is recycled and meets guidelines for permanence and durability of the Committe on Production Guidelines for Book Longevity of the Council on Library Resources.

printed in the United States of America
by Thomson-Shore, Inc.